Dear Dadi

I'd Love to Listen to Your Story

A Guided

to Tell Their Life Story
with a Section for Grandkids to Talk About Them

Contents of This Journal

Section 1: Your Childhood Memories
Stories from your early days—school, games, and friends.

Section 2: Growing Up in Your Era
What was life like when you were a teenager?

Section 3: Family Tales
Family traditions, holidays, and the people you cherish.

Section 4: Your Favorite Things
Hobbies, food, songs, and more that make you happy.

Section 5: Adventures and Travels
Exciting places you've been or wish you had visited.

Section 6: Reflections and Insights
What you've learned about love, kindness, and perseverance.

Section 7: Parenting Lessons
What you've learned about raising children and creating a family.

Section 8: Your Legacy
Messages or advice for future generations.

Section 9: Concluding Thoughts
A place for anything else you'd like to share.

Section 10: A Note from your grandkid
What you've learned about raising children and creating a family.

All About You

Name:

Age:

Birthday:

Address:

Your Hobbies

You are grateful for

Fun Facts About You

Dates important to you

1st

2nd   **4th**

3rd

You are Proud of

Your Favorite ...

Color: ....

Food: ....

Pet: ....

Music: ....

Movie: ....

Season: ....

Place: ....

Sports: ....

Subject: ....

Your Values

Your Dream/s

Section 1
Your Childhood Memories

Your Early Years

1. Dear Dadi, where were you born?

What was your hometown like when you were little?

Section 1
Your Childhood Memories

2.What was your house like back then? Did you have a favorite spot where you'd spend most of your time?

Section 1
Your Childhood Memories

3.Did anyone give you a funny or cute nickname? What's the story behind it?

____

____

____

____

____

____

____

____

____

____

____

____

____

____

____

____

____

____

____

____

3.Did anyone give you a funny or cute nickname? What's the story behind it?

____

Section 1
Your Childhood Memories

Childhood Days

4.What was school like when you were a kid? If not school, what was learning like?

____

____

____

____

____

____

____

____

____

____

____

____

____

5.Did you have a favorite teacher, class, or hobby you enjoyed pursuing? Was there anything special you learned or practiced that you still remember fondly? Were there any subjects you really loved—or ones you didn't like at all?

____

____

____

____

____

____

____

Section 1
Your Childhood Memories

6.How did you get to school? Did anything interesting ever happen on the way?

Section 1
Your Childhood Memories

Games and Fun

7.What games did you and your friends play? Were they different from what we play today?

____

____

____

____

____

____

8.Did you have a favorite toy? Or something you made yourself to play with?

____

____

____

____

____

____

____

____

____

____

____

9.Was there a park or a special place where you all hung out as kids?

____

____

____

____

____

Section 1
Your Childhood Memories

Family and Traditions

10.What was a regular day like with your family? Did you all have any fun traditions?

____

____

____

____

____

____

____

____

11.How did you celebrate birthdays or holidays? Was it different from how we do now?

____

____

____

____

____

____

12.Who were you closest to in your family growing up? Do you have a favorite memory with them?

____

____

____

____

Section 1
Your Childhood Memories

13.Dear Dadi, what's the funniest or most adventurous thing you did as a
   kid?

____

____

____

____

____

____

____

____

____

____

____

____

____

14.Were there any moments that made you laugh so much you still think about
   them today?

____

____

____

____

____

____

____

____

Section 1
Your Childhood Memories

15.If you could relive one happy childhood day, which one would it be, and why?

Section 2
Growing Up in Your Era

1. Dear Dadi, what was life like when you were a teenager? Was it exciting or challenging?

____

____

____

____

____

____

____

2. What did teenagers do for fun back then? Did you have a favorite hangout spot?

____

____

____

____

____

____

____

3. Did you have a curfew, or were you free to do what you wanted?

____

____

____

____

____

____

____

Picnic with Friends

Spend Time with Friends!!

Date

Hangout with Friends

<h1 style="text-align:center">Section 2
Growing Up in Your Era</h1>

Fashion and Trends

4.What was the "cool" fashion when you were a teenager? Did you follow the
   trends or have your own style?

____

____

____

____

____

____

____

____

5.Were there any hairstyles that were super popular back then? Did you try
   any of them?

____

____

____

____

____

____

____

____

____

____

____

____

____

Did you have?

POSITIVE MORNING CHECKLIST
Wake up early
Wash your face
Make your bed
Clean your room up
Drinkwater

Practice

01
Practice

Name The Person who inspires you most

Did you have a daily or weekly habit of reflecting on the things you're grateful for in your life?

And Why?

Do you want to go back with time machine?

Section 2
Growing Up in Your Era

6.Did you ever save up for something trendy, like clothes, accessories, or gadgets?

Section 2
Growing Up in Your Era

Music and Entertainment

7.What kind of music did you love as a teenager? Do you remember the first song or artist you were obsessed with?

8.Did you go to the movies or concerts? What were some of your favorite ones?

9.Was there a TV show, book, or magazine you couldn't get enough of?

Section 2
Growing Up in Your Era

Friendships and Fun

10. Who was your best friend as a teenager? What did you two do together for fun?

____

____

____

____

____

____

____

____

____

____

____

11. Did you ever have a secret hideout or a place where you and your friends liked to meet?

____

____

____

____

____

____

____

____

Section 2
Growing Up in Your Era

12. What's the funniest or most adventurous memory you have with your friends?

____
____
____
____
____
____
____
____
____
____
____
____
____
____
____
____
____
____
____
____
____

Section 2
Growing Up in Your Era

School and Dreams

13. What was school like when you were a teenager? Did you have a favorite teacher or subject?

____

____

____

____

____

____

____

14. What did you dream of becoming when you grew up? Did it change over time?

____

____

____

____

____

____

____

____

____

____

____

____

____

____

Section 2
Growing Up in Your Era

15.Did you ever get in trouble at school or home? What happened?

____

What made it so special?

Anything that made you proud

Year of Accomplishment

Is there anything you would have done differently?

Section 2
Growing Up in Your Era

16.Was there something that everyone talked about during your teenage
   years—like an event, trend, or invention?

____

____

____

____

____

____

17.How was being a teenager back then different from what you see
   teenagers doing now?

____

____

____

____

____

____

____

18.If you could give teenage-you some advice, what would it be?

____

____

____

____

____

____

Section 3
Family Tales

Family and Home

1. Dear Dadi, can you tell me about your family? How many siblings did you have?___________ and what were they like?

____

____

____

____

____

____

____

____

____

____

____

2. What was a typical day like in your family when you were growing up? Did everyone have specific chores?

____

____

____

____

____

____

____

____

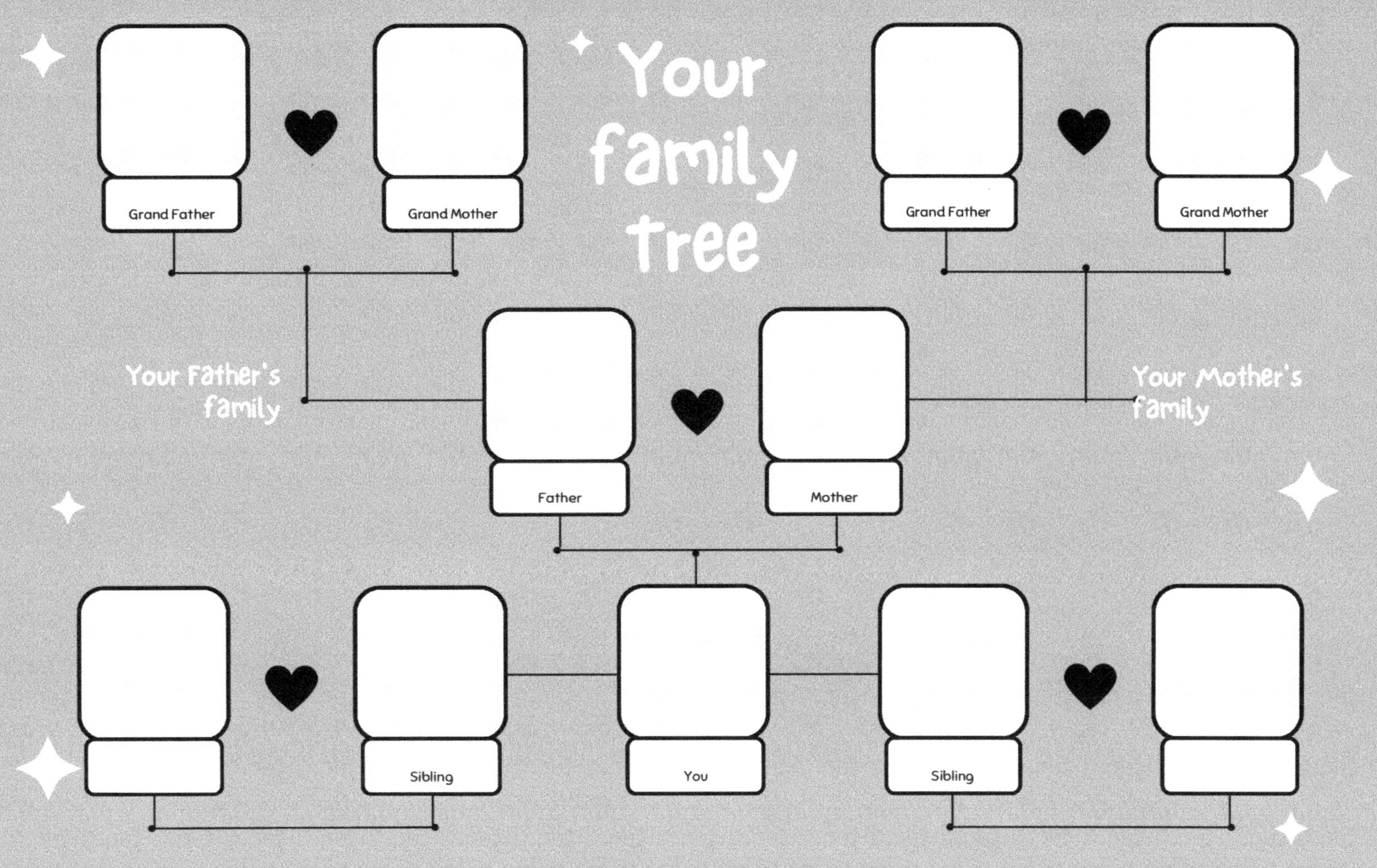

Your family tree
Grand Father
Grand Mother
Grand Father
Grand Mother
Your Father's family
Your Mother's family
Father
Mother
Sibling
You
Sibling

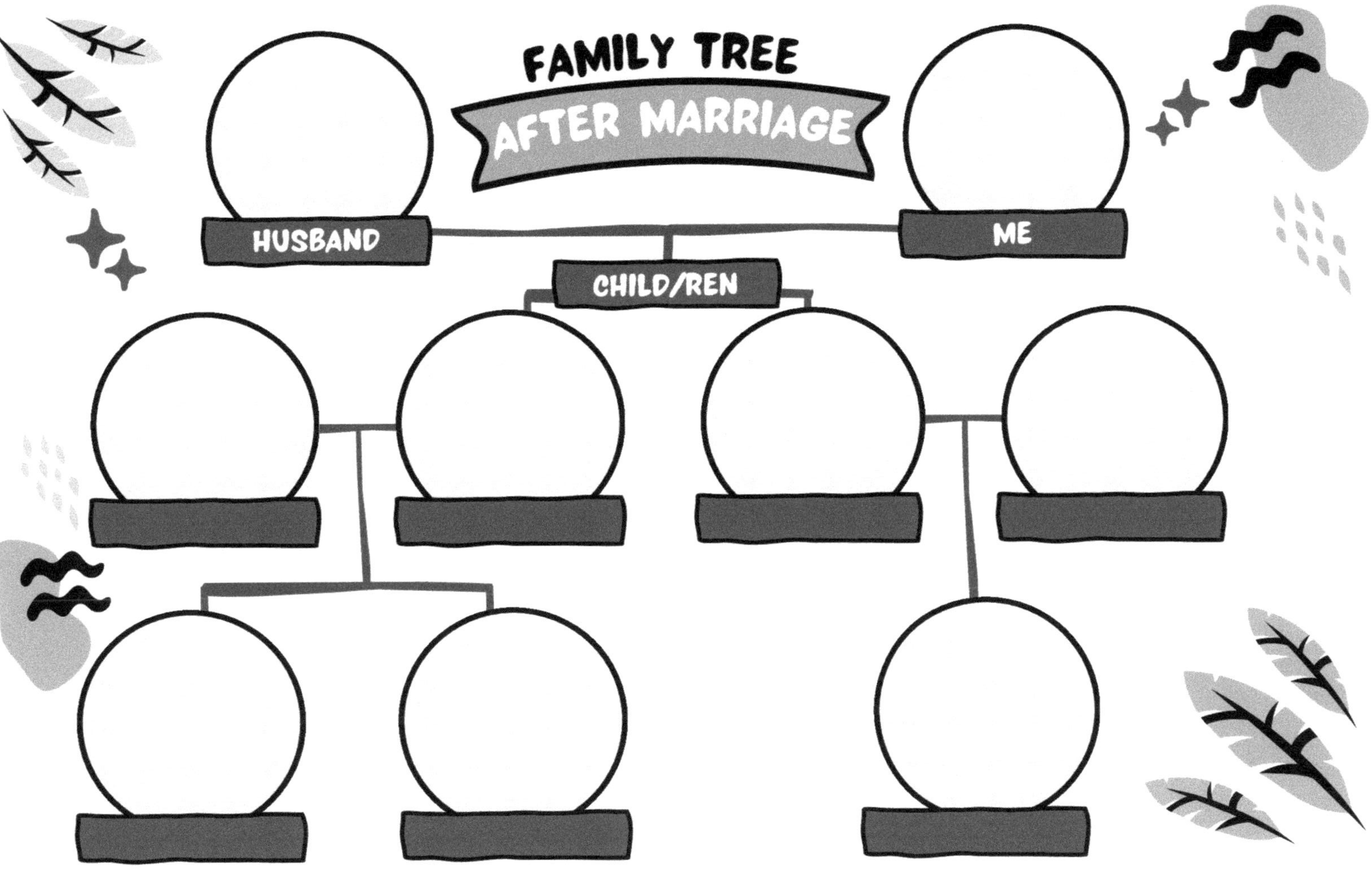

FAMILY TREE
AFTER MARRIAGE
HUSBAND
ME
CHILD/REN

Section 3
Family Tales

3.Did your family have any special traditions or routines that made your childhood memorable?

Section 3
Family Tales

Holidays and Celebrations

4. How did your family celebrate holidays? Was there one holiday you looked forward to the most?

____

____

____

____

____

____

____

____

5. Did your family have a favorite recipe or dish that everyone loved? Who cooked it?

____

____

____

____

____

6. What's the most fun or unforgettable celebration you had with your family?

____

____

____

____

____

____

Section 3
Family Tales

Family Stories

7.Are there any funny, interesting, or challenging family stories that have been passed down through the years? What makes them memorable to you?

Section 3
Family Tales

Family Stories

8.Who was the storyteller in your family? What kind of stories did they tell?

____

____

____

____

____

____

____

____

____

____

____

____

____

____

____

____

____

____

____

____

____

Family Stories

____

____

Section 3
Family Tales

9.Did you have any family pets? What were their names, and were they mischievous?

Section 3
Family Tales

Special Moments

10.Who were you closest to in your family growing up? Do you have a favorite memory with them?

Who is *who in your* family

YOUR MOTHER

Your mom's name is _______________
____
She is _______________ years old
Her job is_______________________
Her favorite color is_______________
Her favorite food is _______________
Your mom is good at_______________
____
Your favorite thing to do with
her is _________________________
____
Your mom loves you because
____
____
You love your mom more than
____
____

YOUR FATHER

Your father's name is_______________
____
He is _______________ years old
His job is _______________________
His favorite color is _______________
His favorite food is_______________
Your father is good at _______________
____
Your favorite thing to do with
him is_________________________
____
Your father loves you because
____
____
You love your father more than
____
____

YOUR SIBLING/S

Your sibling's name/s is/are ______
____
His/her_______________ years old
His/her job is_______________________
His/her favorite color is _______________
His/her favorite food is_______________
Your sibling is good at_______________
____
Your favorite thing to do with
her is _________________________
____
Your sibling loves you because
____
____
You love your sibling more than
____
____

YOUR HUSBAND

Your husband's name is _________
____
He is _______________ years old
His job is _______________________
His favorite color is _______________
His favorite food is_______________
Your husband is good at _________
____
Your favorite thing to do with him
is _____________________________
____
Your husband loves you because
____
____
You love your husband more than
____
____

Section 3
Family Tales

11.Did your parents or grandparents ever share life lessons or advice that you still remember today?

____

____

____

____

____

____

____

____

____

____

12.Was there a family member who always made everyone laugh or brought joy to the house?

____

____

____

____

____

____

____

____

____

Section 3
Family Tales

Family Heritage

13.Where did your family come from originally? Did you hear any interesting
   stories about your ancestors?

____

____

____

____

____

____

____

14.Did your family have heirlooms or special keepsakes that were passed
   down through generations?

____

____

____

____

____

____

____

____

____

____

____

____

____

____

YOUR FAMILY AND YOUR TRADITIONS!

You speak these languages

This is who you live with

These are the Holidays you celebrate

These are your favorite foods

You love your traditions because

Section 3
Family Tales

15.If you could share one thing about your family history with me, what would
   it be?

Section 4
Your Favorite Things

Favorites From Everyday Life

1.Dear Dadi, what was your favorite thing to do when you had free time?

Section 4
Your Favorite Things

2.Did you have a favorite book or story you loved to read?

3.What kind of music or songs were your favorites growing up?

Your Book Tracker

Section 4
Your Favorite Things

Food and Drinks

4.What's your all-time favorite dish or snack? Is there a special memory
   tied to it?

____

____

____

____

____

____

____

____

____

____

5.Did you have a favorite drink or dessert that you couldn't get enough of?

____

____

____

____

____

____

____

6.Was there a recipe your mom or dad made that always felt extra special?

____

____

____

____

____

ALL TIME FAVOURITE
Movies to
WATCH

Singer
Movie Star
Event
Fanmeet
Pop
Star
Dancer
Concert
Your first event
Your favorite movie star
Your favorite Popstar, idol/group
Your favorite Popstar song
Your first Popstar crush
Your favorite Dancer
Have you ever been to concert?
Your favorite singer

Section 4
Your Favorite Things

Special Belongings

7.Did you have a favorite toy, keepsake, or item you treasured as a child or teenager?

8.Was there a favorite outfit or piece of clothing you felt amazing in?

9.Did you collect anything fun, like stamps, coins, or something unique?

Beloved Treasures

Little things that made life special.

What was your favorite toy?

Which area of the house did you love most?

Did you have a special bag or backpack?

What was your favorite outfit or style?

Did you collect anything unique?

Section 4
Your Favorite Things

People and Places

10. Was there a favorite place where you loved spending time—like a park, library, or someone's house?

____

____

____

____

____

____

11. Did you have a favorite teacher, neighbor, or family member who made a big impact on you?

____

____

____

____

____

____

____

____

____

____

____

____

12. Who was your favorite celebrity or role model growing up?

____

____

____

Section 4
Your Favorite Things

Dreams and Simple Joys

13.What was your favorite time of the year—spring, summer, fall, or winter?
   Why?

____

____

____

____

____

____

____

____

____

____

____

14.What's one little thing that always made you smile, no matter what?

____

____

____

____

____

____

____

____

____

____

____

____

____

____

Section 4
Your Favorite Things

15.Did you have a favorite dream or goal you hoped to achieve someday?

____

____

____

____

____

____

____

____

____

____

____

____

____

____

____

____

____

____

____

____

____

____

15.Did you have a favorite dream or goal you hoped to achieve someday?

YOUR LIFE'S PURPOSE AND DREAMS BACK THEN

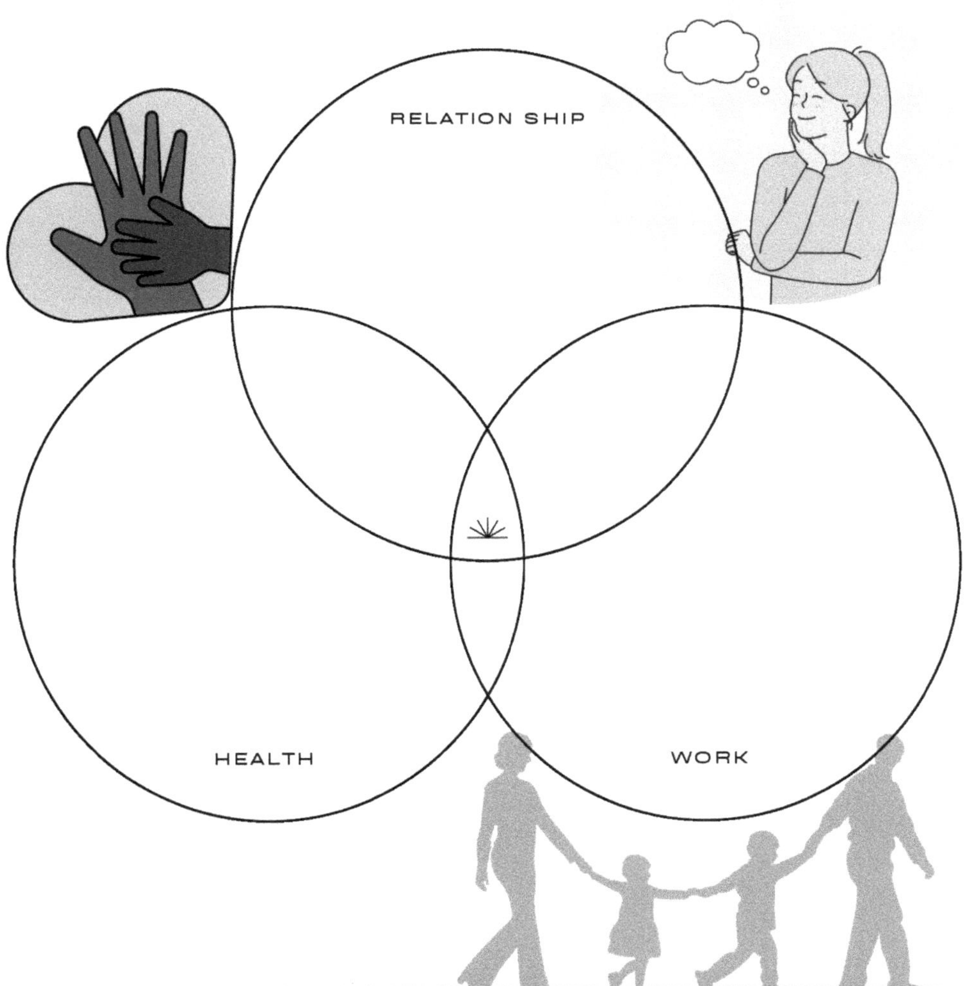

Section 5
Adventures and Travels

Exploring and Wandering

1.Dear Dadi, what's the first big trip you ever went on? Were you excited or nervous? Tell me all...

Section 5
Adventures and Travels

2.Did your family take trips together? Where did you go, and what was the journey like?

3.Was there a special place you loved visiting as a child or teenager?

Section 5
Adventures and Travels

Memorable Moments

4.What's the most exciting or adventurous thing you've ever done?

Memorable Moments

4.What's the most exciting or adventurous thing you've ever done?

Section 5
Adventures and Travels

5.Did you ever get lost on a trip or have something unexpected happen? What did you do?

Section 5
Adventures and Travels

6.Was there a trip you dreamed of taking but didn't get the chance to?

Our best moments!
FAMILY
LOVE AND JOY
FRIENDS

Section 5
Adventures and Travels

Cultural Experiences

7.Did you ever try new foods or meet interesting people while traveling**?**

____

____

____

____

____

____

8.Was there a place you visited that felt completely different from your home?

____

____

____

____

____

____

____

____

____

____

9.Did you bring back souvenirs or memories from your travels that are still special to you?

____

____

Section 5
Adventures and Travels

Looking Back

10.If you could relive one trip, which one would it be, and why?

11.Is there a place you'd want us to visit so we can experience it like you did?

Section 5
Adventures and Travels

12.Did traveling teach you anything important about life or people?

Section 6
Reflections and Insights

What you've learned about love, kindness, and perseverance.

1.Dear Dadi, what's the most important lesson you've learned about love?

____

____

____

____

____

____

____

____

____

____

____

____

____

____

____

____

____

____

____

____

____

____

____

Your Travel Recap
FILM NEGATIVE
FILM NEGATIVE
FILM NEGATIVE
KODAK PORTRA 400
400
53
13
13A
14
14A

Section 6
Reflections and Insights

2.How did you cope with difficult times, and what helped you find your way forward?

Your Life's Learning Reflection

What I learned

Most Challenging Part

How I Overcame Challenges

Something I'm Proud Of

Questions I Still Have

Goals for Next Time

Section 6
Reflections and Insights

3. Were there moments when you felt lost or unsure? How did you find clarity?

____
____
____
____
____
____
____
____
____
____

4.What advice would you give me about being kind to others, even when it's hard?

____
____
____
____
____
____
____
____
____
____
____
____

Section 6
Reflections and Insights

5. What would you have done differently if you could go back, and why?

Do You agree with the following?

If yes why?

Problem Solving Principles

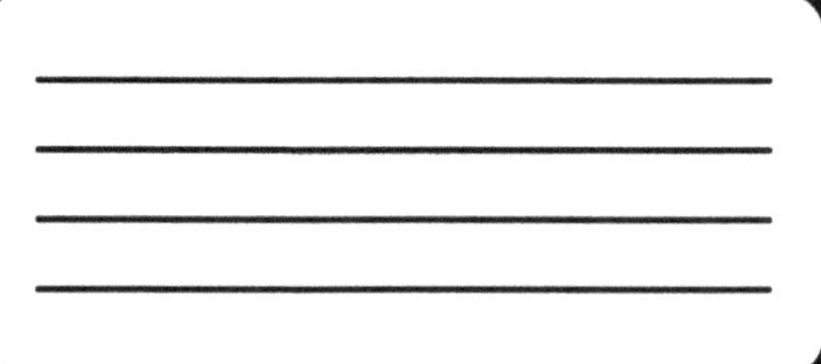

Understand
Do you understand all of the words in the problem?

Plan
Make a plan by gathering your ideas and finding patterns.

Solve
Carry out the plan you created.

Check
Look back and reflect. What worked and what didn't?

Section 6
Reflections and Insights

6.Did you ever face a situation where forgiving someone was the hardest but most important thing to do for your sake?

____

____

____

____

____

____

____

____

____

____

7.What does perseverance mean to you, and how did you practice it in your life?

____

____

____

____

____

____

____

____

____

____

Section 6
Reflections and Insights

8.Who taught you the most about love and kindness?

____

____

____

____

____

9.What's one thing you wish everyone in the world would understand about compassion, understanding, and being mindful towards others and themselves?

____

____

____

____

____

____

____

____

____

____

____

____

____

____

____

How Would You...

Find something important you lost, like your phone or keys?

Take care of yourself when you're feeling unwell and alone?

Fix something that's broken at home?

Stay calm when things don't go as planned?

Section 6
Reflections and Insights

10. What was the hardest decision you had to make, and how did it shape you?

____

____

____

____

____

____

____

____

____

____

11. If I want to live a good life, what's the one lesson you think I should always remember?

____

____

____

____

____

____

____

____

____

____

____

LET'S TRY PROBLEM SOLVING

Briefly write about how you should react in the following situations of past in present time:

You dont know how to answer the question.	
Your best friend is away from school.	
You have no one to play with outside.	
Your friend doesn't want to play the same game as you.	
Your classmate falls over and hurts themselves.	
You don't think you did well in a test.	

Section 7
Parenting Lessons

What you've learned about raising children and creating a family.

1.Dear Dadi, what was the best part about being a mom or dad?

Section 7
Parenting Lessons

2.Did you have any rules or traditions in the house that you always followed?

____

____

____

____

____

____

____

3.What's one thing you think every parent should make sure to teach their kids?

____

____

____

____

____

____

____

____

____

____

____

____

____

____

____

Timeless Parenting Lessons

Section 7
Parenting Lessons

4. When parenting got challenging, what helped you stay composed and work through it?

____

____

____

____

____

____

____

____

____

____

____

5. What's the funniest thing you experienced as a first-time parent that still makes you laugh?

____

____

____

____

____

____

____

____

____

Section 7
Parenting Lessons

6.Was there any advice about parenting that you got that really helped you
   out?

Do you believe in
Mindful Parenting?

Fostering Emotional Intelligence in Your Child

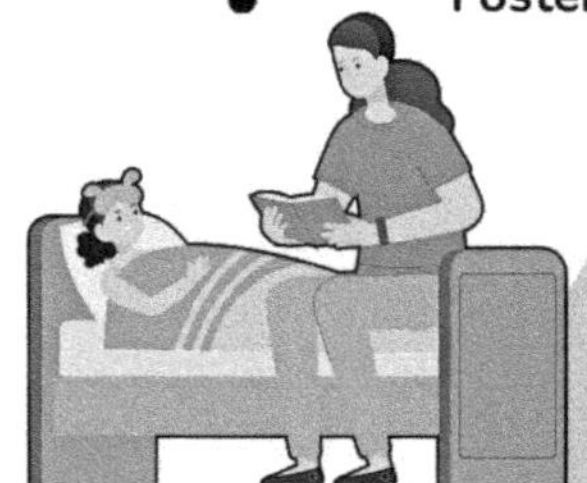

Create Calm Rituals

Talk, listen, and understand. Effective communication builds strong bonds.

Model Mindfulness

Be the mindful mirror. Children learn best by observing. Model mindfulness in your daily life.

Celebrate Successes, Big and Small

Acknowledge achievements. Celebrate both big milestones and small victories to foster a positive self-image.

Shopping Together

Help them appreciate the small and big things in life

Brush the teeth together

Reassure them that your love is not based on their achievements but simply because they are who they are.

Read a story together

Share meals, stories, and laughter together. It's the memories of connection that last a lifetime.

Play games

Let them fail, learn, and grow from their mistakes without fear of judgment.

Section 7
Parenting Lessons

7.How did you find time to take care of yourself while raising us?

____

____

____

____

____

____

____

8.What was your favorite thing to do with us when we were little?

____

____

____

____

____

____

____

____

____

____

____

____

____

____

____

____

What did your
Me-time for Self Caring
look like while parenting?

Section 7
Parenting Lessons

9.Looking back, is there anything you'd do differently as a parent?

Section 7
Parenting Lessons

10.What's the biggest lesson about love you learned from being a parent?

Section 7
Parenting Lessons

11.When they didn't listen or messed up, how did you handle it?

Section 7
Parenting Lessons

A place for anything else you'd like to share.

12. Do you think parenting rules can work for every child, or should they change to fit each child's unique personality?

____

____

____

____

____

____

____

____

____

____

____

____

____

____

____

____

____

____

____

____

____

____

Section 7
Parenting Lessons

13.Can you recall a moment when observing your child taught you an unexpected and valuable lesson?

Section 7
Parenting Lessons

14.How did becoming a parent change your perspective on the world?

____
____
____
____
____
____
____
____
____
____
____

15.What's one thing about parenting you believe remains timeless, no matter the generation?

____
____
____
____
____
____
____
____
____
____
____

Section 8
Your Legacy

Messages or advice for future generations

1.Dear Dadi, what's the one message you'd like to leave for our family?

____

____

____

____

____

____

____

____

____

____

____

2.If you could share one piece of advice with me about living a happy life, what would it be?

____

____

____

____

____

____

____

____

____

____

Section 8
Your Legacy

3.What do you hope people will remember most about you?

HOW WOULD YOU LIKE TO BE REMEMBERED?

Section 8
Your Legacy

4.If you could tell your younger self one thing, what would it be?

____

____

____

____

____

____

____

____

____

____

____

5.What's one tradition or habit from your life that you think our family
   should always keep alive?

____

____

____

____

____

____

____

____

____

____

____

Morning Prayers

Daily Family Meals

Festive Celebrations

MUST-DO RITUALS FOR...

Community Service

Seasonal Cleaning

Bedtime Reflections

Section 8
Your Legacy

6.What do you want future generations of our family to know about where they come from?

Section 8
Your Legacy

Messages or advice for future generations

7.If you could write a "life motto" for us to follow, what would it say?

____

____

____

____

____

____

____

____

____

8.What does "leaving a legacy" mean to you?

____

____

____

____

____

____

____

____

____

____

Section 8
Your Legacy

9.Is there something about our family history you want to make sure we pass down?

____

____

____

____

____

____

____

____

____

10.What's the most valuable lesson you'd want me to teach my children someday?

____

____

____

____

____

____

____

____

____

____

Section 9
Concluding Thoughts

A place for anything else you'd like to share.

1.Dear Dadi, I know we've talked about a lot, but is there anything we haven't talked about that you've always wanted to share**??**

____

____

____

____

____

____

____

2.Is there a memory or story that makes you happiest, but haven't shared yet?

____

____

____

____

____

____

____

3.Is there something you wish more people knew or understood about life?

____

____

____

____

____

____

____

____

Section 9
Concluding Thoughts

4.Do you have a dream or wish for our family's future?

____

____

____

____

____

____

____

____

____

____

5.What's a piece of wisdom you've kept close to your heart that hasn't come up yet?

____

____

____

____

____

____

____

____

____

____

Section 9
Concluding Thoughts

6.Is there anything you've always wanted to do but never had the chance?

Section 9
Concluding Thoughts

A place for anything else you'd like to share.

7.What's one thing about your life you're most proud of?

____

____

____

____

____

____

____

____

____

____

8.What simple joys in life have meant the most to you?

____

____

____

____

____

____

____

____

____

____

____

____

Section 9
Concluding Thoughts

9.Is there a song, quote, or poem that describes how you feel about your life?

____
____
____
____
____
____
____
____
____
____
____

10.Is there a message you'd like to leave behind just for me?

____
____
____
____
____
____
____
____
____
____
____
____

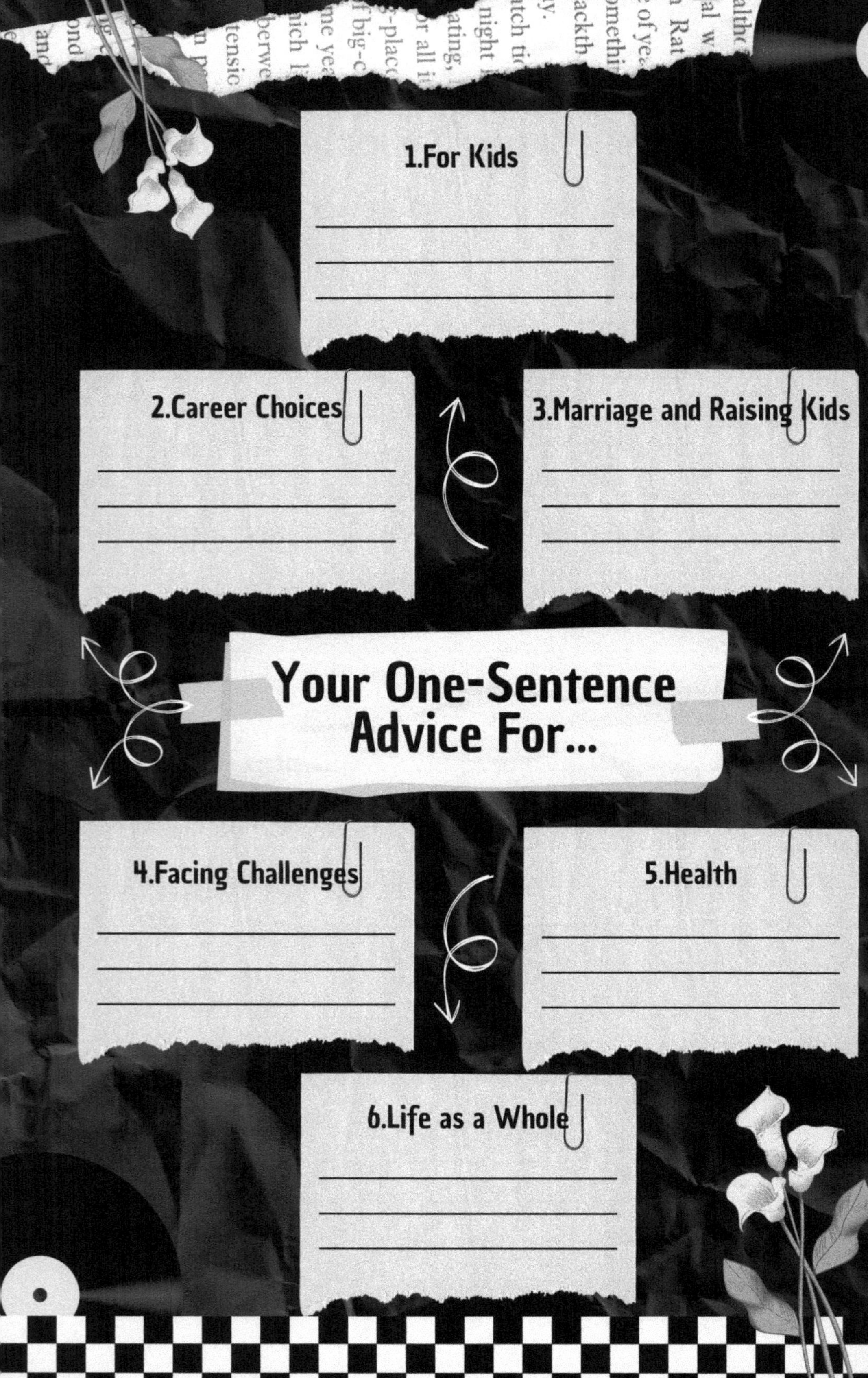

1.For Kids
2.Career Choices
3.Marriage and Raising Kids
Your One-Sentence Advice For...
4.Facing Challenges
5.Health
6.Life as a Whole

Section 10
A Note From Me to You

Dear Dadi,

After reading all your wonderful stories and memories, I've realized just how amazing you are. I'd like to share some of my thoughts with you. Here are a few things I've been thinking about as I've learned more about your life:

1. Dadi, I feel we are like/unlike each other because __________________

____

____

____

____

____

____

____

____

____

2. The most interesting thing I like about you is __________________

____

____

____

____

____

____

____

____

____

____

Section 10
A Note From Me to You

3.I never thought you could do this _______________________________

____

____

____

____

____

____

____

____

____

____

4.One thing I wish I could have seen or experienced with you is _______________

____

____

____

____

____

____

____

____

____

____

____

Section 10
A Note From Me to You

5.Your story about__________ made me feel ________________________________

____

____

____

____

____

____

____

____

____

____

6.I've learned __________ from your stories, and it's something I'll always
remember.

____

____

____

____

____

____

____

____

____

____

____

Section 10
A Note From Me to You

7.If I could go back in time with you, I'd want to see _______________________

____

____

____

____

____

____

____

____

____

8.One question I still want to ask you is _______________________________

____

____

____

9.I'll always remember you because_____________________________________

____

____

____

____

____

10.I hope one day I can be as ________________ as you. ________________

____

____

____

____

____

Conclusion
A Heartfelt Goodbye

Dear Dadi, thank you so much for sharing all of these wonderful memories and life lessons. Your stories have helped me understand you better and have given me so much wisdom to carry with me in life. I feel lucky to have you in my life, and I will always treasure the lessons you've passed down.

No matter where life takes me, I will carry your words in my heart and try to live by them every day. Thank you for being such a special part of my journey, and for always being there for me with your love, kindness, and wisdom.

I will always remember you, and your legacy will live on through me, through the stories I share, and the way I live my life.

With all my love,
[Your Name]

You and Me